# Thoughts
# I Left
# Behind:

Collected Poems
of
**William H. Roetzheim**

Level 4 Press.com
San Diego, CA

This book was illustrated by
William H. Roetzheim

The author would like to thank the following individuals for their help in reviewing and critiquing this work: Gene Auprey, Carol Buchholz, Ruth Casey, Jackleen Holton, Adina Jerome, Christopher McDonald, Stephen Scaer, Martha Shea, and Larry Weisman as well as all of the participants in the various on-line poetry forums who have offered comments on individual poems, and especially the folks at the Poetry Free For All (PFFA) poetry forums; and Marshall Harvey for help with copyediting the manuscript. "Stretch Marks" was initially published in Oberon's Fall 2005 edition. "Fertility Doll", "Dinner at the Diner", "Fading into Background", "The Seven Heavenly Virtues", "Stretch Marks", "The Seventh Circle", and "Shadow Friends" have won poetry prizes/recognition in the Milford Fine Arts Council National Poetry Contest, Writers Challenge, Faulkner Society Poetry Award, Oberon Prize, Pagan Poetry Contest, Saturday Writers One Page Poetry Contest, and the Baltimore Science Fiction Convention Poetry Prize.

Published by Level 4 Press, 13518 Jamul Drive,
Jamul, CA 91935-1635 USA.
www.Level4Press.com

*Library of Congress Cataloging-in-Publication Data*
*Thoughts I Left Behind: Collected Poems of William H. Roetzheim*

*by William H. Roetzheim*
*p. cm.*
*1. Poetry 2. English poetry. 3. American Poetry. I. Roetzheim, William H.*

Library of Congress Control Number: 2005903198

This book is printed on acid-neutral archival quality paper.
Printed and bound in Canada.

To Sue a friend of mine
+ she has been a friend
for a long, long time with Love
Bety

10.08

Dedication

To my wife Marianne -
because thoughts of her are always close at hand -
never left behind.

# Table of Contents

## Table of Contents

# Table of Contents

## Welcome

I'm sure you must be tired.  The journey here
is long, the roads are dark and poorly marked.
They're little more than ruts in places where
most travelers fear to brave the woods.  But here,
I'll take your bags and pour a glass of wine.
Let's pull our chairs up to the fire.  I've waited
all my life to share some thoughts with you.

# Thoughts While Dying

## Recruit[i]

While lost, I toddled off to join the Navy,
with hopes I'd learn to fly and find my Willie
in aviation's cradle, Pensacola.
I took the choo-choo through Mobile and joined
with other kids who left their cribs to rattle
sabers, pacify the populace,
fly from carriers, and diaper
the ragheads who were less than animals.
Running, we learned songs of death and glory,
found our role was but to do and die,
crash and burn, buy the farm, but first we do
it to the other guy.  A sea of green
with bobbing sheen of pink that bobbed in time
to stomping feet and ribald songs of whores
and pimps, sung anapest to match our steps.

I knew a gal who was dressed in red,
she had a parking meter on her bed.
I knew a gal who was dressed in black,
She made her living lying on her back.
Sound off . . .

## First Time

She lies there impatiently, lips pouting,
one knee raised, and glances at her watch.
Her finger commands me to the bed.
I throw my shirt down, flex my pecs, bulge my biceps,
strike a pose as I reach into my wallet.

My fingers tremble as I tear the foil packet,
a Trojan Supra: extra large.

She watches my hands shake,
as circus music begins to play,
and she begins to smile.
The rubber clown's hat
held between thumb and forefinger,
is getting bigger and bigger.
The room goes dark.  From her eyes,
a pencil spotlight follows my hands.

The more she stares
        the more I shake
                the larger it gets

The more she stares
        the more I shake
                the larger it gets

until I find myself
grasping the shield, putting it over my head
and unrolling the protection over my body.

I see her laughing now.
I curl up, suck my thumb,
while she hums nursery rhymes and takes me inside of her.

## American Carrier[ii]

City floats by—
yellowjackets sleep now.
ozone before rain.

Distant Roman Legions,
shout a silent warning.

# Dreams[iii]

I study books on astral dreaming,
seeking a way to be with you.

## Beware of "Friends":  A Villanelle

Beware of friends with cautious love advice.
I sing a song of warning from the heart.
They kill your love with words, as trust departs.

With arm on shoulder, walking you apart
they offer words of wisdom, so concise.
Beware of friends with cautious love advice.

"It's up to you," they say, but then impart
an evil thought, a fear, to be precise,
to kill your love with words, as trust departs.

With honey words, soft eyes, they sink a dart
with poison for the human sacrifice.
Beware of friends with cautious love advice.

"If it were me," they say, "I'd play it smart."
"Don't be a fool," they cry, "You'll pay the price."
They kill your love with words, as trust departs.

As they plant seeds, destroy your counterpart,
their evil game is done, crushed hearts their vice.
Beware of friends with cautious love advice,
that kills your love with words, as trust departs.

## A Poem for Minimalists

In learning from museum's art,
with old masters I made my start,
but wandering the abstract floor
I noticed then, that less is more.

Poetry's art, art, poetry—
a sudden thought occurred to me,
my mission now was to create
the shortest piece to contemplate.

Select a topic, universal,
keep it short and very terse, so . . .
my first attempt was just five words,
Read with feeling, the heart stirs:

"Unending love, always and forever."

Pretty short and not too bad,
but must be shorter, just a tad.
My second try, the words were two,
capturing feeling with words few.

"Unending love"

But still too many, still too long,
shorter yet I made my song.
To say the same thing, just one word.
The shortest poem you've now heard:

"Marianne"

## Stretch Marks

You lie beside me,
snoring lightly, nude and tan,
your breasts relaxed.  My eyes are drawn
to spider webs of lacy white along
your side, across your breasts.
The delicate patterns branch and weave,
swoop down the curves
and glide across the planes and slopes,
embossed and subtle decorations,
flesh on flesh,
The lines entwine, and seem to spell our love,
our family, our thirty years together.

## Fasting

I'm fasting for a week, no food
and only water to drink. I think
of Jesus' forty days secluded
in prayer. The goal that I pursue,
less holy, getting my gut to shrink
(to be a Greek God when I'm nude).

Though weak with hunger I call on will
to exorcise the demon's lure
of chocolate shakes and burgers, grilled
with bacon, fries and free refills.
Just watch my butt become demure
from lengthy strolls on this treadmill.

A test of will, the time too slow
as food controls my every thought.
I wonder, should I learn to sew,
give up and let my pants out? No!
I can do this, though I'm distraught,
six days and twenty-three hours to go.

# Rafting

i.
Our group put in at Miracle Hot Springs
to raft the lower Kern River.  Dry bags
were filled with watches, rings, and other things
we should have left behind.  We helped to drag

the rafts, those helpless whales, to water where
they came alive, their breathing sides our seats.
To learn we all linked arms into a square
and swayed to bow then stern, like those who meet

new friends in beer gardens.  We learned to row
in time, to dip and pull as one, our feet
gripped to inflated thwarts.   A slow tempo
pulled us along, as paddle's steady beat

advanced the craft through our first run down Wallow
Rock, a class three gate, then down Lost Shorts
and Silver Staircase, easy when we followed
the metered pace demanded by this sport.

ii.
We abandoned ship
to float down a lazy stretch of river,
reclined as if in lifejacket lounge chairs that drifted
through the tranquil shade of overhanging trees—
and the river embraced me.
I watched my feet floating before me, the world slowly turning;
and the river thrilled at the touch of my feet.
A hot spring gushed from the river bank,
                              filling the air with the smell of sulfur
and tingling my skin as I momentarily drifted through it's warmth;

and the river absorbed the water from the hot spring.
The tepid stream meandered past a herd of grazing cows,
then as I spun further,
a blue heron stared at me, cocked his head,
flew over in a cloud of water droplets;
and I was the river, and these trees, springs, animals, birds
                                    were all my children.


The sound of rough water ahead grew louder,
and climbing back aboard was difficult, so one-by-one
our guide grabbed under our lifejacket shoulders
                                    and threw us into the raft
like flopping catfish
pulled from the river by our gills.


iii.
Again we rowed in time, "front two," "front two,"
"front one," "front three," "back one"; our strokes called out,
called while we spun through Pinball, Possum, Horseshoe.
Class three, class four, we ran them all without

a fall because we stayed in time with feet
locked down. At last we pulled to river right,
beyond an Eddy line our rubber fleet
approached a cliff of granite laced with quartzite.

iv.
On the edge
of the jumping rock ledge

alone
but for nudges
from behind

**23**

the water below
sparkles, like distant concrete.

v.
And next, the roughest run of all; class four,
four plus with lots of hair.  This smoker called
and so we locked our feet and left the shore,
and headed for the roar of Sundown Falls.

We saw the chute and heard the drop, the first
raft wrapped around a sieve—that tree embraced
them like a drowning man whose hands submersed
his rescuer with claw-like grips.  We braced

and cart-wheeled past the tree, then saw the hole.
"Front three," "Front two," "STOP!"
We reached the edge, tipped down, started to roll,
"Back three," "Back Hard!" "Dig In!" "STOP!"

We swirled past, over the falls, the raft
a snake below my legs, it curled and spit,
recoiled and struck, then diving down our craft
was gone, I rode just foam until we hit

below, and there I found the raft still locked
in place.  And so I find free verse is nice
when floating down the stream, but facing rocks
and falls find only meter will suffice.

# Working

## Dunkin' Donuts

First jobs are best jobs.
Proud in my paper hat while
scrubbing pots and pans.

## Shoe Store Stock Boy

Wanting to peep up
skirts, but stacking endless shoes
for less than one week.

## McClean's Car Wash

Rummy with friends while
occasional customers
interrupt the game.

## Booz Allen and Hamilton

People problems solved
Machiavellian style—
then bigger sharks came.

# Help Desk

No, don't transfer me to
international help,
they referred me to you.
No, don't put me on hold.
I've held since he was seventeen.
I've threatened, reasoned, cajoled.
My effort's no good, in vain,
the problems remain.

Busy signal.
Disconnected.
"Wrong number, Dad."

## Artificial Life

I saw a demonstration
of a simulated girlfriend.
The computer imitation
carried on a conversation.
Over time, she might disrobe.

I saw an exhibition
of a proudly prancing puppy—
well, a robotic rendition
with a puppy-like cognition.
Over time, he might learn tricks.

I saw an Internet creation
of a planet and it's people,
an artificial nation
with disaster and starvation.
Over time, you might be King.

I watch
the clicking clock.
Sign
the dotted line.
Begin
to spin the chair.
Sharpen pencils
again
and again.
Over time, I too
might come alive.

## Fatal Error - Core Dump[iv]

How do you stop a neuron from firing? They fire on their own and create random patterns and random thoughts. So I'm living in a world of random, swirling electrical impulses that fly around in my brain. Yesterday I saw my brain through a special camera that looked through the optic nerve in the back of my eyeball directly to the brain tissue. The brain was white, full of energy, it looked searing just like a miniature sun in the back of my eye. While I was waiting I read an article in the Reader's Digest special edition (large type). The article described a woman who underwent an operation that required that her heart and brain be stopped (they cut into her skull). She watched her operation from above, then went down a corridor toward a bright light. She was met by dead relatives. Her uncle guided her back to her body. Reentering her body was like jumping into a cold swimming pool.

Sometimes life is like that. Or perhaps it's more like sitting in a bathtub filled with ants. They crawl out of the drain in a steady stream and cover you, the walls of the tub, everything around you. The itching and small pain is terrible, but if you move you know they will sense you are here and attack in mass, killing you under the carpet of ants.

Last night I had a dream I was walking down a street when a plane wheeled around and set up for a napalm bombing run. I knew it was happening and wanted it to happen. I quickly lay down in the gutter next to the curb and covered the back of my neck with my hands. The napalm was dropped and as it hit me it felt like water from a cold swimming pool caressing my hands, and back, and legs.

Maybe I'll start running and build my way up. First 15 minutes, then another 5 minutes each day. Eventually I'll get to the point where I'm running 24 hours per day. I'll run on a treadmill, but in my mind I'll be running down an Aztec trail with a message for the king. Run, run, run, run, I'll just do that forever. Keep running away, farther away. But even in my fantasy, when I'm done running I open my eyes and I'm still in the same place. Even when I run away, I can't get away.

## Opera Season

I couldn't attend the opera this season.
The thought of your seat empty next to mine
was too much to bear.
I put our tickets in a kitchen drawer,
then mentally buried that drawer with you.

Like Therese Raquin I am haunted
by your ghost in every corner.
Like Rigoletto, that which was most precious to me
was taken away from me.
Like Butterfly, I confidently wait for our reunion
in this intermission between life and death.

001*205143 - 1/53

DATUM 22.10.05

ČAS 19:00

BUDOVA Stavovské divadlo

PŘEDSTAVENÍ Therese Raquin

MÍSTO I. galerie vpravo

ŘADA 1

SEDADLO 53

CENA 200.00 Kč

## Horned Lizard

I watch it watch me.
Its push-ups are cute,
but its dark drill instructor eyes
wipe that grin off my face.

The name fits it well.
The spikes along its head
and barbs along its back, legs, and tail
bristle and threaten
like a Stegosaurus.

When attacked it raises
the blood pressure in its head
until small blood vessels burst,
spitting blood from its eyes
to confuse its predators.

In my mind it grows to thirty feet,
six thousand pounds,
stares down at me with those same cold eyes.
Suddenly I'm sure that dinosaurs are not extinct,
but are hiding among us,
waiting.

# Landscaping

We don't have the money to landscape yet,
so our three acres are native chaparral—
ecologically sound "xeriscape".

Red Tail Hawks surf on afternoon updrafts.
Crows play tag, pretend to fight.
An owl makes ghostly groans as she seeks a mate.
Coyotes howl throughout the hills.
I stand naked on our balcony,
and howl at the moon with them.
California quail call in the canyons.
Rabbits nibble apologetically.
Lightning-fast fence lizards race on the patio.
An early morning chorus:
House Sparrows, Song Sparrows,
Brewers Sparrows, Lark Sparrows.

Like Walt Whitman,
I long to pull it all into my bosom,
to be part of it.
Soon I will send forth my men and machines
to destroy all that is around me.

## The Zen of Yardwork

*Thanks to Al Zolynas*

I'm chopping down wild tree tobacco,
Nicotiana glauca.
The broad leaves sway overhead,
offering cooling shade,
supplication to the executioner.
Like those of old, I accept the payment
in return for a clean cut with a sharp ax.
The yellow clusters of flowers,
golden trumpets,
announce my approach.
As I pause to sharpen my ax once again,
a shimmering green hummingbird
pauses for a sip from the flower,
and the tobacco obliges.

## Fading into Background[v]

The murmurs were the first to go,
those eavesdropped conversations
moving here and there within a crowded room.
And soon I lost discussions
from across a crowded table
at loud and boisterous weddings,
gone to background noise
like waterfalls, and for my part
just nods and smiles,
nothing but nods and smiles.

And then my wife as translator,
"What did she say?"
"What did he say?"
Until I found
it didn't really matter what they said,
when nods and smiles will say enough.

## Christ's Face Found in Photos from Mars

The headline answered questions seldom posed
in supermarkets.  Why was Christ no longer
close to me?  Why had our dialogue
become a monologue, then silence, deep
as altar candles snuffed, their curling smoke
like question marks?

Perhaps he's gone to Mars
to rest from saving sheeplike souls on Earth.
It seems unfair that he should go away
and leave me here, although I must admit
that even God His father had a day
of rest.  At least I know just where he's gone.

## Old Storms

I think it might be El Nino, perhaps
it's global warming, but the weather now
is faded, weak and old. It seems to me
the lightning tries, the thunder shakes, while wind

and rain drops fly, but all to no avail;
for I recall the smell and sound and sight
of healthy storms, of youthful storms that might
drown roads, send light right through closed eyes, and dance

with monster trees until those trees collapsed
onto their knees, too tired to go on.
The storms today inspire far more yawns
than screams. We're tired old men who long for youth.

## Shadow Friends

I worship shadows like my daughter worships sun.
I don't mean those so crisp and dark
beneath a noon-time sun,
or shadow soldier squads
before a picket fence.  Those underneath
a harvest moon are more my style; the way
they hide and watch
from low bushes, then dance around
the lifted skirts of swaying trees,
like witches in a forest glen.
I've lured them home with low-watt bulbs
in gargoyle sconces under overhangs.
At night my friends uncoil
on walks and walls, then call me to their yard
to stroll and see my life in grays and blacks.
And in my den the shy ones come to watch
me read by candlelight.  They come, pull back,
grow bold, then sly; so while I sip my scotch
and swirl the ice I'm not alone. I'm not
depressed.

## Old Man in the Distance[vi]

A cemetery's not a place of sorrow
for young boys who invade, tiptoe through dares
of life on death.  They gasp at granite graves
with chiseled dates that tell of babies dead
at birth, and young men
dying during World War One,
for families lying side-by-side
since nineteen-eighteen—no doubt
Spanish flu.  Then too
those clever phrases left behind,
those final grasps at permanence.

I once crawled from my bedroom window,
ran three blocks through moonlit streets,
the way cool clay on my bare feet.
I hopped the graveyard wall
to laugh at death in mist and fog.
While walking silent,
slightly scared,
I looked through halos round a light
and saw an old man standing there.
His hair was thin, his belly bulged,
and as he turned and walked my way
I swore I'd seen his face
before, a face like mine,
and still today I see that face, that face
I know but do not know, now even closer.

## Winter Sanctuary[vii]

I pull my coat closed against night's
winter wind. The snow demons howl,
and prickle my thighs.
I crunch through deep snow
to the massive fir tree,
my childhood friend and sanctuary.

I lift her skirt and climb within,
then close the bough and hug my friend.
The voices call, but damn them all,
I'm tired now and those
who need me plead in vain,
my time is served.

The limb is cold beneath my gloves,
old joints protest as bark slides past and slowly
up the trunk I climb. The tree transporting,
quivers her excitement,
branches grasp,
delighted.

From up high the voices fade,
and looking down I watch
the wind and snow erase
the tenuous track cross rocks and earth.
The wind dies; silence wraps
us both.

## Wading Pool[viii]

When just a boy, we had a kiddy pool,
light blue with dinosaurs around the sides.
One day I found that I could float face down
in womb warm water, drift in dappled sunlight
under elm tree canopies, peaceful
until a sudden scream and grab that flung
me sparkling skyward into mother's arms.

Today the kids
and grandkids tempt me up the ladder standing
like a walker someone set atop
the side of their above-ground pool. They laugh
and splash and circle round to swirl the water,
making currents, rivers, rapids, now
a whirlpool that pulls me faster, faster,
feet just barely touching down, and in
the center of the pool a funnel forms.
It seems to call me down, a need to fall,
give up and let that force take me inside,
down deep inside this tunnel calling me.

# Dust Unto Dust[ix]

There's something reassuring about death.
As my body decays,
the other evidence of my existence
will likewise fade.

My carefully collected books, wide-screen TV,
Mercedes Benz SLK, and other belongings will be
sold, distributed, discarded, given
away. Before my body is gone, the physical traces
I left behind will equally be hidden.

Memories of me will last longer:
friends and children will remember me fondly;
grandchildren only vaguely.
Specific memories will evaporate,
and after another generation, maybe two,
all memories of me will dissipate.

Death brings the anonymity of a post office box,
allowing me to slip through the coming centuries
silent and unobserved.

# Burial Objects

## Down Comforter

My grandmother gave me a comforter,
green plaid and filled with down.  It held me tight
and whispered while we snuggled
on dark winter nights,
or sat with me to count the trucks
that leapt like sheep across the patches rubbed
through clouds of ice on dormer window panes.
But then the godlike parents came,
and stole my friend,
a gift from them to little Sis
in her new bed.  I cried and pled, then locked
myself behind the bathroom door, prepared
to die, to end it all with suicide
by drinking cup after small Dixie cup
of water, throwing empties to the floor.
I would have made it too except that Dad
removed the hinges on the door.
But back behind danger
the comforter just seemed to laugh and point,
wrapped around the one who held
it now, the one it loved instead of me.

## Cardboard Boxes

Toboggans made from boxes carry friends
down slopes of grass and sand, end over end

to heaps of laughing laundry.  Take away
both ends and step inside the passageway

with one or two beside and start the scream
engine in your assault tank. Children seem

just like hamsters, running, pushing, clawing
up the side to keep it moving, crawling

forward over driveways, lawns and sidewalks,
pausing briefly just to rest and talk.

Add extra boxes, carefully arrayed
in tunnels, stacks, and rooms—climb in you've made

the perfect fort with cardboard windows, doorways,
watchtowers and secret rooms. Then play

inside, the peerless place for battles, candy
banquets, sharing secrets, even dandy

for first kisses.  Today I bought a wide
screen toy, then crushed and threw the box outside,

# Telescope

Late at night
when the air crackled
and the world paused,
I liked to leave my bed.
I rode a plastic telescope
over snow covered fields
and up the rough gray bark of oak trees.
Cracking the frost-covered escape hatch,
I could draw in the cold
sting of night.  Islands
of distant incandescent light
beckoned their mystery.
Occasionally
a plane passed overhead,

and I hitched a ride
through golden portholes.
Today,
I find it difficult to explain to my wife
why I sleep with the window cracked,
even on shivering nights.

# Centerfold

I put away the scotch tape and sit on the lab stool,
watching as the other students straggle in and sit down.

Mr. Baumgarten turns sideways,
rolls through the door,
pokes his glasses,
hitches his pants,
and adjusts his bright red suspenders.

My eyes flit with anticipation to the silver canister
containing the now rolled up screen
as Baumgarten waddles to the overhead projector
with a fist full of transparencies.

The room is lined with jars containing
screams and shivers.
Tape worms, organs,
and parasites of all shapes and sizes.
In the front, we can reach inside,
grab the heart in our hand,
and yank it from the chest

of a plastic cadaver.

Mr. Baumgarten stands on tiptoes to pull down the screen,
as I struggle not to laugh in anticipation of his reaction.

The room is full of surprises.

## Slicing Watermelon

The best are shoulder-width and cheap, sold just
before they get too ripe.  The sacrifice
is placed lengthwise on old newsprint.  I thrust
the blade into the flesh, cut down and slice

crosswise until I'm left with two inch disks.
I toss the ends, then one by one I sever
flesh from rind with circle cuts, then whisk
the rings of rind away.  And now the clever

steps.  The flesh is placed upon a plate.
I slice and pull the center piece, filet
of watermelon.  Then I cut and rotate
"round the outer side, about halfway,

(beyond the seeds), and take this outer part.
What's left has rows of seeds like spokes, with seedless
wedges held between.  Cut them apart
and keep the wedges, toss aside the needless

spokes, a pile of undesired life,
the inconvenience excised with my knife.

# Fertility Doll

Returning home I brought my wife some gifts,
among them was a carved figure—an ugly
woman with huge breasts and bigger belly.
Hawaiians said her name was Hi'iaka.

She stood beside our bed and watched, her eyes
reflecting red in candlelight, her shadow
dancing with obscene and naked joy
to hear Bolero by Ravel, to hear
the primitive music of need and want.
And in one month my wife told me that she
was pregnant after trying for so long.

We loaned her out to Loni, who was pregnant
that same month.  And then the breathless call
when Hi'iaka had the same results
for Betty Lou, after four years of trying,
crying, clinics too.  But now my laughing
wasn't easy, now I found that I
was queasy when I thought of Hi'iaka's
naked dancing, watching with those eyes
that seemed to glow.

I know, I know she's just
a doll and not a god, not like my god,
the western god that toppled her and all
her kind two hundred years ago, although
she dances on our wall, her shadow leaps
and falls, and quietly she plants her seeds
of pagan thought, of faith in ancient gods.

## The Four Seasons

The green Van Briggle vase starts plain, a Roman
shape more tall than wide, but flowing from
the sides four women grow with abdomens
as handles, thrusting out to overcome

the prison holding back their lewd desires.
Their feet are trapped and melted while their heads
are fastened back by hair to neck. Attired
in sheets they pull to cover breasts, that shred

of decency betrayed by pouting lips
and wanting eyes. Each looks away, one east,
south, west, and north. Perhaps each thinks the grip
might soon relax, and she will be released.

## Navy Flight Jacket

It's made of muddy brown leather, with wool
trim at the wrists and waist that's holed by moths
and slightly soured by stale beer.  And here
it's scorched, a cigarette fell from a sleeping
hand to brand the leather sleeve.  The worst
is garish patches everywhere: here black
submarines on green oceans, there winged
jaguars about to pounce through lightning bolts.
One shows a plane, an S3 Viking, now
useful just to ferry parts and mail.
An inside pocket sized to hold a pilot's
thirty-eight is now sewn shut to fix
a tear.  I know that I must throw it out.
They all agree, but still I hide it here.

## Skeletons in the Closet

It started with a bird, the carcass stripped
some months ago by bugs and wind until
just bones remained.  I made a shoebox crypt
and kept it on the closet floor.  Roadkill

was next, a bloated cat I hid outside
under a bush, so mother earth could strip
the flesh from bone.  But then I found a dried
cat skull was all she left, and so I clipped

it to a hanger by its ears.  I crammed
the bones of a small dog onto a shelf
behind the shoes.  I tried to stop, was damned
to sin as skeletons much like myself

came to my door, just barely knocked, then strolled
right in.  The nights with them were free and wild,
I would remove my skin and neatly fold
it on the bed.  Around me all the skulls just smiled,

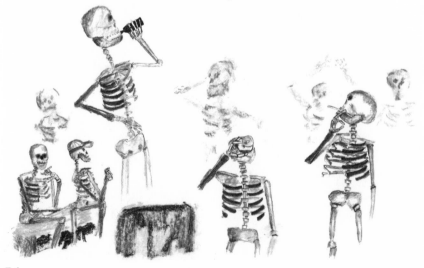

their clacking claws would offer drinks, we'd sing
and dance, smoke pot and talk of inhibition,
of how I'll leave this life, leave youthful flings
behind, grow up and get some real ambition.

# Haunting San Diego

## Florida Canyon

Arrayed before me, three pictures I found
but didn't take.  The first is oaken stairs
of rough hewn boards, descending down around
the canyon walls.  You spin; your shoulders bare,

your smile still shy.  The second photo shows
you squatting down to feed a squirrel, hand
outstretched and breasts exposed. The squirrel low;
its tail erect and full.  The third looks planned.

I see the trail's end, you lie across
our worn-out quilt, draped near a pumpkin vine
with yellow buds.  You turn your head and toss
your hair, a naked pistil lying supine.

Reluctantly I gather them and stack
them up, then carefully I put them back.

# Kate Morgan[x]

You almost left in eighteen-ninety-two;
shot through your skull, but you survived
to haunt the Hotel Del,
a later day Qandisa,
San Diego growing while you watched
through second floor windows.
I know you now.
I've studied sordid details
from your past, the sexual abuse,
affair with Reverend May,
moll to Tom, and now
you scare the guests
with steps and parlor tricks.

A group of friends came with me visiting
the other day, room three-three-twelve reserved
well in advance.  By candlelight and incense
we recited Poe and Baudelaire,
then some late night conversation,
speaking slowly through your Ouija board.
And yes those dreams!  Those wild dreams
of you and me, your panting chest,
our icy love,
your tender eyes and bony clutch.
The evening ended much too soon,
but ghosts as lovers cannot last.

## Balboa Park

With paper towels gone, the cardboard tube
displays a rounded view, as scene by scene
I scan the park.  Above a palm frond screen,
a naked girl holds up a roof, her boobs

flop down as arms hold up a beam, her face
patient, resigned.  Below, an old man plays
a tarnished sax—plays "Summertime" and sways
slowly.  He nods as quarters fill his case.

A pause as a clock tower chimes the time,
the bells ring slow and lingering tones, they ring
and float their mournful notes to climb on wings
and drift away.  The sax resumes and I'm

pulled back to cardboard tube and small round view.
I lie back, look up, and stare at space
above. You lean toward me and as your face
appears, my small round world is filled with you.

## Bungee Jumping in the Angeles National Forest

The Lost Bridge stands five miles beyond
the nearest road.  The mountain gorge
is granite, quartz and copper, forged
by God who used tectonic force

and polishes with water still
one hundred feet below the bridge.
My kids and I stand on the ridge
and see it all: the concrete arch;

the rocks and waterfalls below;
the red platform that's one foot square
and juts precariously on air
from tenuous links to stone.

A silent stare, then back across
the bridge to huddle close, afraid
at last, determined too, they've paid
the jump fee in advance.  I'm here

to watch, too old and shy with fear
to date this whore of Babylon
who dangles cords between her pylons,
and offers flight and fright for just

one leap of faith.  Now one-by-one
they climb across the rail and stand
like baby chicks.  They swing their hands,
then leap away to "soar like eagles."

And you would think that was the end,
but each rebounded near again,
then far, then near, friendship, disdain,
needing, then not, though each approach

was not so here and more of there,
"til only specks remained below.
Then I walked home alone, too slow
to keep up with the kids ahead.

## San Diego Zoo

My first date with the gal I'll love and marry
six months hence, and first trip to the zoo
as well.  Her overalls more customary
for the farm than city dates, but through

the sides my view of breasts behind white cotton
twists my eyes and pushes pants till I
relate to horny primates trapped, forgotten,
left to beat frustration, spit and cry

at pointing crowds.  We stroll while holding hands,
then stand before a cage of devils from
Tasmania.  Two fight on limbs that span
the cage's crest.  One falls and lies knocked dumb

or dead, the other scampers down the tree:
nudges the unconscious one and grips
her waist, humps her quickly, then turns and flees
as she wakes up. "You're all the same." Anne quips.

# Roetzheim Manor

## Music Room

The room is filled with carved wood chairs, no two
alike.  Rest here where swans proffer their necks
to hold your arms, or there where lion heads
stare out, their paws braced firmly on the floor.
Lithesome statues offer glowing globes,
while paintings act as portals, famous women
staring out.  They seem to dance as candles
beat in time to blues played on the grand
piano.  French doors open wide to spas
and pool and waterfalls.  What luxury
to sing the blues among such opulence.

### Library

One hundred years of polish speak to me.
An English Lord and Bach chorus call from
the candlelight reflections on the wood.
The chairs are large as parent's laps, full backed,
and covered with a rough brocade. The walls
are floor-to-ceiling leather books. I pull
one down and feel the pebbled skin, the ridges
on the spine, the gilded edges smooth
and cool—an old lover that calls to me.

## Pub[xi]

This room's a safe retreat that's used by friends
to talk philosophy and reminisce.
The oak throughout is welcoming much like
an English pub I once enjoyed.  At night
I feel the spirits of the trees run through
the grain in floor and bar and furniture,
then swirl up these oaken colonnades
that flank the countertop.  The green
marble that forms the shelves was once algae
in ancient shallow seas.  Pressure and time
may harden scum to beauty, it appears.
We're stocked with fine brandies, cognacs, and yes
of course the best in single malt scotch whiskey—
but these two shelves display my love of rare
American bourbon, none aged for less
than twenty years.  That cherry humidor
contains cigars to conjure days when Britain
ruled the world, and much was left to be
explored, intrigued, conquered, destroyed.  You'll find
I don't come here often.  When blue flames float
above the surface of a small shot glass
entire worlds may burn quite suddenly.

### Disco

It has its own power panel, more ampers
than most houses I've owned.  The vaulted beams
are covered with bright colored lamps, spotlights
that seem to dance and blink and morph in time
to beating drums.  At night they shine through arched
windows to climb those hills across the street,
to march along the ridge, then swing back down
to dazzle dancers feet.  Five thousand watts
drives Klipsch speakers to form a pool of liquid
sound that fills the room, to drown the crowd
in beats like undertow.  Last Halloween
my kids were home, an eerie scene of circled
masks was formed, and all four danced for me
in their own style: ballet on point, a mime,
gyrating club go-go, and hula hoop.
But while they danced the fog machine began
to cycle on and off, and slowly fog
obscured the view, until just shapes remained—
just shadows far from my reality.

## Guest House

This house will be your nest during your stay.
It's the original Victorian
farmhouse that ruled these hills, a gray
old dame who broods by night, but in the day

she wears her stained glass windows like those jewels
that sparkle on arthritic joints, those cruel
reminders of past youth.  Historians
tell us this was a stage coach stop, a school

for wayward boys, and then the olive king
lived here-the one who introduced the can
of olives to America.  His plan
to grow Maurinos like in Tuscany

left a legacy of olive trees
throughout the county, trees that bloom each spring
and live one-thousand years, but nobody
gathers the fruit—now just messy debris.

## Cottonwood Falls

A mile or two off Sunrise Highway, down
a stone and dirt trail we hear the falls.
My Saint Bernard and I drive up from town
each month or so, and walking I recall

each dog that came with me before: protective
Kip, inquisitive Snickers, wild Lady,
Whitey the hunter, sad Ellie, reflective
Patches, and shy Matada walked this shady

path with me. Acuna's lived well past
his time, and I suppose that's true for me.
Much like my dogs, my spouse and friends have passed,
left just the two of us, and so now we

come here alone to limp along this path,
responding to the falls which sound possessed
by distant voices, murmured calls too frail
to hear clearly; but hearing them we press

against the fading light to try to see
what lies behind. We sit down by the stream,
his head upon my lap. He nods at me
while I read verse aloud, or so it seems.

# Wild Animal Park[xii]

We wait to board the bus, to watch the wild
through dirty windows as we drive around
the habitat.  The door opens, we pile
aboard and take our seats without a sound.

I'm squeezed between a panda on my right
and rhino on my left.  The panda's large
and soft and middle-aged, pants stretched too tight
and shocking pink.  She monitors discharge

into the bay for the Coastal Commission.
The rhino has tattoos across his arms,
his shoulders bulge, he's a radar technician
who lifts weights on the side.  He left the farm

to join the Navy many years ago,
and learned a skill he uses still.  A mother
reads while childlike monkey dynamos
run up and down, throw napkins at each other,

peek over seats to say hello.  Outside
the homeless men lounge in the sun. They chat
and laugh, some sleep in shade.  "We're caged," confides
Panda, "They're free in their wild habitat."

## Alpine and Pacific Railroad

The Alpine and Pacific Railroad track
goes round a loop through Leroy Athey's yard,
and though you don't go very far in space
the journey takes you to a distant time
when railroads ruled the land, the pace of life
was slow and every boy loved every train.
He has a blacksmith shop and builds his parts,
and entertains the kids with railroad lore
while driving them through tunnels, over bridges,
through trees—and all without requesting fees
of any kind except a smile and eyes
that open wide with a new love of trains.

## Carlsbad Flower Fields

For years I've driven by, admired the quilt
of color over hills in Carlsbad,
so finally I took the tour.  The Flower
Fields are known around the world, the source
of bulbs that look like baby octopi
but are in fact rhizomes, the dried out roots
of Giant Tecolote Ranunculus.
The fields are segregated into red,
yellow, purple, orange, and white brocade.
The workers pull those blooms that dare to venture
where they don't belong, and thereby keep
the gene pool pure.  But in the border zone
I found some plants with rainbow hues, and thought
their wild kaleidoscope was best of all.

## Sunset Cliffs[xiii]

The view is somewhat blocked by those in line
in front of me,  but leaning left I see
the sandstone ledge ahead, just past a sign
that reads "Danger: Unstable Cliffs."  The sea

a distant green as we shuffle through waves
of sun amid the tiny flies that like
our sweat, or lick our salt.  No longer paved,
our path is sand which scuffs my shoes, a hike

in dress wingtips. I crook my arm, lean down,
and sniff my pit. It's bad, but then I'm not
the only one. I reach the edge, see brown
of cliffs meet surf below.  A tiny spot

is someone walking on the beach. I frown
as Paul steps off the edge. Without a peep
Jim follows Paul, then Frank. I don't look down
but trust in Frank, now far below, and leap.

# Coronado Bridge

I paint the bridge and love the way
she stands two-hundred feet

above the bay, with one foot touching
Coronado's shore,

the other planted deep upon
the poor of Logan Heights.

In Coronado fancy homes
and high priced cars are proof

they have a life in Pleasantville.
In Logan Heights you'll find

a slum of drugs and gangs, a life
in Peasantville.  Eight times

a year some fool will stop their car
and jump—a suicide.

More than two hundred since my first
day on the job.  The funny

thing about it is, the cars
that stop are not the junker

cars you'd think I'd see, but Porsches,
Jags, and Mercedes.

## Twilight-Steele Canyon Golf Course[xiv]

I looked to you for inspiration, read
poems from your "Leaves of Grass", but still
I'm blocked, my mind a blank, and so instead
I grabbed you by the spine and sensed a thrill

as pages flapped. I took you for a walk
and showed you manicured fairways, and perfect
greens. A caddy passed, you turned and gawked,
I pulled you back to here and now, then checked

him out myself. I showed you plastic flowers,
concrete paths by artificial lakes
and waterfalls. But still no help, your dour
face stared out from the book, refused to wake

and help me out. We crossed a bridge above
the rough, a canyon filled with wild plants.
I must have slipped although you seemed to shove
and push past me to tumble down, enchanted

by the weeds below. I struggled down
the canyon slope and reached a hidden valley
where . . .

Behold!
See the yellow and brown butterflies sip from the purple flowers
        The flowers shaped like tiny cornucopia,
See the rabbits tremble as they nibble
from the young green grass,
        The grass a seven-fold harvest from last year's seeds,
See the stream feeding the Spanish oaks
with sweet, cold water

The stream overflowing its bank to offer water for all,
See the oak as it shades and protects all that is below,
and everything is as it should be, and always will be!

## Mount Helix

The amphitheater atop Mount Helix
is made of boulders, gifts from mother earth
as if the mountain top itself gave birth
to seats and aisles and stage.  The rocks and stones

themselves cry out the songs of Jesus Christ,
as well as King and I, and Caravan,
Fiddler on the Roof, and Music Man.
The stage is closed, but overhead—the stars.

# The Book of Sevens, Part 1

## The Seven Deadly Sins

### Pride[xv]

Dad gave me freedom in most things, but he
forbade one thing.  I could not buy or ride
a motorcycle.  God!  This one taboo
seemed so unfair.  He would be mortified
to know my friends all rode, and took me out,
our tires hissing down serpentine roads,
the candy apple paint aglow.  Devout
son that I was in other ways, doubt sowed
by those friends led me down the path to see
how he sought to stop a transformation
from boy to man.  He would not hear my pleas
that this meant manhood, not just transportation.
    And as I bit the apple, only then
    saw pride drive me from Eden into sin.

### Envy

Insistent ivy grows most anywhere,
finds cracks in solid stone, solidifies,
substantiates. It's nowhere, then elsewhere,
then everywhere. Ruthless roots occupy
the dark, dank flaws found in submissive stone—
weaken, crumble, and turn the stone to dust.
It climbs tall trees, soon choked and overgrown,
the sunlight blocked with green leaves of mistrust.
Rats run and breed in ivy's cooling shade,
safe in the twisted maze of stems and stones.
They leave their nest at night, run soft, invade
your home to steal from you, leave you alone.
　　Thus green which might be pretty from a distance,
　　will grow and slowly kill with its persistence.

## Greed

My trophies stand on walnut shelves, and brag
of deeds in business, sports, and literature.
I dust the past, squint at the plaques, my rag
caressing memories so they'll endure.
When five years old I stole some paper bags
from Jimmy's hardware store.  At twelve I swiped
a watch from Sears, at seventeen could brag
I kept two hundred cash—the check mistyped.
And now I vaguely recollect awards,
accomplishments that fade with passing years,
but every detail of my greed is stored
and without help appears both fresh and clear.
    So trophies try to keep my good alive,
    but guilty thoughts need nothing else to thrive.

# Lust[xvi]

We sit across a small wrought iron table.
Your low cut dress befits a noble woman.
"I'm just a prostitute", you say.
The flower waterfalls cascade from gables,
beams and walls, the cafe Schober mute,
except for violins.  We drink within
Monet's Giverny.  Red, green, blue and pink
scream out in riotous hues, begin
to flow around and overwhelm.  I blink
and shake my head.  Can what I see be real?
"It's just a cafe."
I really am inside a Monet oil.
I grab my pen to capture this ideal
moment, look for words that will not spoil
    this dreamlike magic feeling, pull me back
    to midlife gray and virtues that I lack.
"This is all just a poem," you whisper.

## Anger

A bang of smoke surprises me.  My hand
extends, touches the wall and feels a glare
of heat.  The unexpected fire demands
attention.  Cautiously I sniff the air
to find the source.  I recollect no fault
right here, no prior problem, yet now sparks
begin to fly and blind, I cannot halt
the flames.  The circuits trip, then sudden dark.
I shiver, turn my back to wait it out.
"The problem's over," you complain. "What's wrong
with the TV?  And now I'm cold without
the heater.  Why the silence for so long?"
     Eventually circuits reset and I'm
       the same, my feelings back unchanged.  Most times.

## Sloth

I'm testing out a new device.  It feeds
through optic nerves and cochlea direct
to deep inside my cerebrum.  I'm freed
to live alternate lives, I can connect
to my choice of six-hundred-sixty-six
channels.  I sit with the remote control,
the cable snaking here and there, and fix
my eyes as broadcast demons beg, cajole
and try to sell the golden calf.  I flip
my life, or so it seems, to sexy friends
enjoying love, or lust, or evil quips,
made simple, helping me to comprehend.
    And so I live a thousand times and places
    without living, or seeing living faces.

### Gluttony[xvii]

I sit inside a whorehouse in Pompeii,
taste the wine in empty vats, and leer
as risque ghosts parade down stone runways.
I gorge on long buffets washed down with beer,
belch, then start again after a quick
side trip into the vomitorium.
Thank God it's all a dream, a mental trick.
I haven't sinned, and every ghost succumbed
to falling ash in ages past, and now
they burn in hell, a second burn, because
they worshipped Roman gods.  And yet somehow
I know that this is false, and always was.

> Our God includes all other gods, and when
> your actions harm noone, they are not sins.

# Responses to the Dead

## Giambologna

### Rape of the Sabines

We sit on cement seats,
in the Piazza della Signoria,
sketchpads on our knees.
The young Roman's feet straddle
his cowering rival, ignoring pleas as
he carries off the maiden
daughter.  I've blocked out forms,
and begin shaping and shading
the muscles, the hair, the fingernails;
The marble eyes stare as I try
to capture their expression.
My God, the detail.
I look over the shoulder
of the dark haired girl from France
but she's having problems too.
I look left at the blond boy from Belgium,
but he's trying to sneak the solution
from my sketch.  The museum guard walks among us,
arms behind his back, bending forward
for a better view,
tongue clucking its judgment.
I look up again for help from Giambologna,
but he just chuckles, claps the dust from his hands,
and walks away in victory.

# Emily Dickinson

## 249

*Wild Nights—Wild Nights!*
*Were I with thee*
*Wild Nights should be*
*Our luxury!*

*Futile—the Winds—*
*To a Heart in port—*
*Done with the Compass—*
*Done with the Chart!*

*Rowing in Eden—*
*Ah, the Sea!*
*Might I but moor-Tonight—*
*In Thee!*

## Response

We sat around a fire and drank Merlot,
A California wine called "Two Buck Chuck"
by those of us that shop at "Trader Joe's."
When someone asked, "If I had to be stuck

in Jimmy's mountain cabin for a night
with anyone except my wife, who would
I choose?" I thought of you, images right
and verses tight with clarity I should

achieve but never will.  But more, I want
you on the night you wrote this piece, the panted
words fresh from your pen.  And lest God taunt
you for your wish I'd have the light be slanted

such that I appeared to be the one
inside your mind when this piece was begun.

# William Ernest Henley

## Invictus

*Out of the night that covers me,*
  *Black as the pit from pole to pole,*
*I thank whatever gods may be*
  *For my unconquerable soul.*

*In the fell clutch of circumstance*
  *I have not winced nor cried aloud.*
*Under the bludgeonings of chance*
  *My head is bloody, but unbowed.*

*Beyond this place of wrath and tears*
  *Looms but the Horror of the shade,*
*And yet the menace of the years*
  *Finds, and shall find, me unafraid.*

*It matters not how strait the gate,*
  *How charged with punishments the scroll,*
*I am the master of my fate:*
  *I am the captain of my soul.*

## Response

Why is it I can't be like you,
When faced with woes from pole to pole?
Somehow I haven't got a clue,
but you are always in control.

You are the master of your fate:
You are the captain of your soul,
While I'm uncertain, gay or straight?
And by the way, what is the goal?

But like a mantra I repeat
Your words to help inspire my life,
the words allowing no defeat,
the spirit's triumph over strife.

I say it often, night and day—
but one more thing before we're through,
a simple question if I may:
"Did all this really work for you?"

# A.E. Housman

## They Say My Verse Is Sad:  No Wonder

*They say my verse is sad: no wonder.*
*Its narrow measure spans*
*Rue for eternity, and sorrow.*
*Not mine, but man's.*

*This is for all ill-treated fellows*
*Unborn and unbegot,*
*For them to read when they're in trouble*
*And I am not.*

## Response

Thank you for this, which I uncovered
to find help from the dead
for pain of unrequited love.
("Get lost" she said.)

You sent it forward ninety years,
but it gave little cheer.
Instead of helpful verse I'll try
another beer.

# Christina Rossetti

## When I am Dead, My Dearest

*When I am dead, my dearest,*
*Sing no sad songs for me;*
*Plant thou no roses at my head,*
*Nor shady cypress tree:*
*Be the green grass above me*
*With showers and dewdrops wet;*
*And if thou wilt, remember,*
*And if thou wilt, forget.*

*I shall not see the shadows,*
*I shall not feel the rain;*
*I shall not hear the nightingale*
*Sing on, as if in pain:*
*And dreaming through the twilight*
*That doth not rise nor set,*
*Haply I may remember,*
*And haply may forget.*

## Response

When I am dead, my dearest,
Plant a young oak tree,
Bury my body beneath
So I can nourish and flow
Into the wood and leaves.
Then sit beneath the shade
As I watch over you.

# Robert Greene

## Content

*Sweet are the thoughts that savor of content;*
*The quiet mind is richer than a crown;*
*Sweet are the nights in careless slumber spent;*
*The poor estate scorns Fortune's angry frown.*
*Such sweet content, such minds, such sleep, such bliss,*
*Beggars enjoy, when princes oft do miss.*

*The homely house that harbors quiet rest;*
*The cottage that affords no pride nor care;*
*The mean that "grees with country music best;*
*The sweet consort of mirth and music's fare;*
*Obscured life sets down a type of bliss:*
*A mind content both crown and kingdom is.*

## Parody

Soft is this bed. I like my Hyatt room
while friends camp out or stay at Motel Eight.
Soft are my hands. I'll watch my garden bloom;
my job? fill in amount, and name, and date.
Such luxuries, such toys, such food, such bliss,
rich folk enjoy, but paupers tend to miss.

My Mercedes that rides with quiet speed;
My front row seats to country music's best;
My mansion with a staff to meet my needs;
And if I'm bored, a cruise to take a rest.
It's true that poverty's no sin, but this—
my happy life of leisure—this is bliss.

## Robert Louis Stevenson

### Requiem[xviii]

*Under the wide and starry sky*
*Dig the grave and let me lie:*
*Glad did I live and gladly die,*
*      And I laid me down with a will.*

*This be the verse you grave for me:*
*Here he lies where he longed to be;*
*Home is the sailor, home from sea,*
*      And the hunter home from the hill.*

## Response

Embracing death, you penned this verse,
and told me here, death's not a curse:
Jump to your grave right from the hearse,
    Lie down with a will, you write.

Your words are somewhat transcendental,
and yet the problem's fundamental.
As Thomas said, I won't "go gentle
    into that good night."

# William Shakespeare

## Sonnet CXXXVIII

*When my love swears that she is made of truth,*
*I do believe her though I know she lies,*
*That she might think me some untutor'd youth,*
*Unlearned in the world's false subtleties.*
*Thus vainly thinking that she thinks me young,*
*Although she knows my days are past the best,*
*Simply I credit her false-speaking tongue:*
*On both sides thus is simple truth suppressed:*
*But wherefore says she not she is unjust?*
*And wherefore say not I that I am old?*
*O! love's best habit is in seeming trust,*
*And age in love, loves not to have years told:*
   *Therefore I lie with her, and she with me,*
   *And in our faults by lies we flatter'd be.*

## Response

I tell my love that she smells nice, her hair
looks good today, I like her slinky outfit.
I say she's young as when we met, declare
she's lost some weight.  She says, "You're full of shit."
Perhaps like you I should compare my love
to summer days,  and promise that my verse
will grant immortal life.  Or point above
and claim a love that fills the universe,
and us two souls sky-bound.  "I think I'll pass."
is how she would reply.  So Will, did you
have luck with lies?  I'd rather cup her ass,
undo her top, stop chattering and screw.
    Perhaps our love would grow if we could "lie",
    and through those pleasant lies, be gratified.

# Walt Whitman

## My Legacy

*The business man the acquirer vast,*
*After assiduous years surveying results, preparing for departure,*
*Devises houses and lands to his children, bequeaths stocks, goods,*
*funds for a school or hospital,*
*Leaves money to certain companions to buy tokens, souvenirs of gems*
*and gold.*

*But I, my life surveying, closing,*
*With nothing to show to devise from its idle years,*
*Nor houses nor lands, nor tokens of gems or gold for my friends,*
*Yet certain remembrances of the war for you, and after you,*
*And little souvenirs of camps and soldiers, with my love,*
*I bind together and bequeath in this bundle of songs.*

## The Business Man replies:

You wrote your verse,
(If you can call it that) without meter, and worse, no rhyme.
No skill to impress me
after a lifetime reading masters every night.
It looked to me like jotted thoughts about your life, the fight
of North and South, delight in your indecent love—
a shameless, lazy life
of watching then recording things.

I worked six days a week, twelve hours a day,
obeyed the law, and built a fortune with my hard work,
then in my death donated all to my High School.
They named a gym to honor me, but then those fools
renamed the school for you.

# Bob Marley

## To the Tune of "Is this Love?"

I come from snorkeling,
Buck Island, then Trunk Bay.
My catamaran
climbs then falls into salt spray.
I play Bob Marley,
and the seagulls beat in time.
They float beside me,
then they turn and swoop and climb.
I drink rum, I drink rum,
I drink rum, I drink rum and I'm laughing.
While gulls hover and pivot and fall down the wind
to the water,
where they skim almost swim as they play
in the air, and I'm, I'm photographing.
I play Bob Marley,
and the seagulls beat in time.
They float beside me,
then they turn and swoop and climb.

# Lost Souls

## Grandpa Johnson

In the photo you hug us tight.
You're kneeling in your jeans and checkered shirt,
my brother hugs you back, like a puppy.
I pull back, my eyes focused on the camera,
the person in the second reel of the horror film
who senses something is wrong.

Looking at the picture,
I can't smell the Wild Turkey,
or hear the screams of rage—
there's nothing but a giant hug.

When I was old enough I killed you
for your weakness,
buried you where you belonged,
then ignored your pleas
from within your tomb.

Now that I'm older
with grandchildren of my own,
and find there is room for two
inside the sepulcher.

## Grandpa Roetzheim

Grandpa was a carpenter,
like all the Roetzheim's back in Germany—
generation upon generation.
A beam extended there from birth,
to tell you who and what you were,
the plane on which you built your life.
But Dad refused

and sought a different level—
so Grandpa saw their paths diverge,
a bevel pointing out, away.
So Grandpa shrugged then hammered out a book,
hand drawn with notes,
enamored with the thought
of propagating skills
for future Roetzheim carpenters.

His drills and other tools were stored inside,
the handmade chest locked tight,
and pushed toward those future
generations. Like a joist
it crossed two worlds,
supporting hopes unvoiced
but locked within the frame
of leather bound dreams.

I'm not a carpenter,
but found the trunk and thought I saw a sinking ark
of wood and nails, old things
shrinking slowly.
I passed it to my son,
but kept the book.

He sold the tools,
that is except a few
on kitchen walls,
and yesterday I cleaned my house
and found to my dismay
I'd lost
the manuscript,
and now my Grandpa's hopes are gone.

# Regina[xix]


That night she sang in "Music Man",
while proud Papa stood in the wings,
nodded and clapped, more beaming than
the spotlight, watching as she scanned
backstage for me.  My star offspring

had little time, but moved upstage
as Conroy crooned in "Bye Bye Birdie,"
my front row seat now empty.  Pages
flipped as programs swirled and aged
in minutes, turning faded, dirty

before I even read the lines.
She sang solo in "Runaways,"
I craned from orchestra seats assigned
by her.  Her voice and blocking shined
through the proscenium archway.

I watched Les Mis from mezzanine,
she moved stage right, and though nineteen
she sang the lead and stole the scene.
I clapped and cheered, remained unseen,
then watched her leave in a limousine.

In balcony for "Much Ado,"
(obstructed seats a hindrance)
I watched her cross, and always knew
stage terms are from the point of view
of actors, not the audience.

## Harold

In the yellowed photo you sit in an old jeep
covered in dirt, your uniform crumpled,
your eyes mysterious.
There is no door.  You wave the photographer off
as you reach down to start it up.

I drop the camera and scramble back.
You laugh as you drive off,
my legs stinging in the gravel and dust.

This is the only time I'll meet you.
But later, in your daughter's body,
I'll fall in love with those eyes,
raise our children,
and grow old with you.

## Unrestrained Love[xx]

You left your mess around the house again.
Your love is everywhere!  I found it thrown
across the made up bed.  Can't you restrain
yourself and keep it in?  I hear the phone

and know you're sending love down wires to friends,
while mixing love with gourmet meals.  I found
a pile in cupboards stocked with food.  I send
love back, but then there's more.  With kids around

it's worse than ever, jumbled love throughout
the room, dig down there's more love underneath.
The kids bring problems home, but then lookout,
an avalanche of love, and lost beneath?

those problems.  Well, I guess I just will bear
the mess-my heart is lost in here somewhere.

# Uncle Rob[xxi]

Sharecropping Indian land, he grew string beans,
his brown truck bounced from field to field,
through brown clouds of dirt that swirled around
brown clouds of shuffling men.
Steel sheds in fields covered shapeless dresses
that bowed and cowed and crawled within.

He made a fortune.

His invention
was a mobile factory—
a dinosaur creation crawling over dusty fields
while eating beans in front and dropping crated,
packaged beans behind.
E coli women did the work
from deep within the beast's intestines.

## Ellie

Searching lights along the road
seem to call your name and whistle.
What do the other searchers know of a loyal friend?
You lie half in, half out,
too weak to move.
I cradle your head,
rest your snout on my leg.
Your eyes look at me as if to thank,
but then turn blank.

## Lisa

A friend emailed me an article,
describing your wiccan wedding.
I always knew you were a witch at heart.
I do not care about your life.
I printed the article from my computer,
then tore it up and threw it away,
because you are not important to me.

I've done that many times,
over the years.

I think I'll do it again right now.

## Helicopter Boy

My daughter keeps the boys
anonymous, junk mail that flows
from letterbox
to kitchen counter,
then into the trash.
They have no names, but slide right by
with labels vague as OCCUPANT:
Wilderness Guy,
Motorcycle Dude,
and Surfing Kid.
I don't meet them, or learn their names,
but like a widowed man who slowly reads
the ads and magazines,
I take what tales she gives.

I know that someone's been discarded,
returned to sender,
when I find a potted plant.
Wilderness Guy is now a yellow Pothos,
Motorcycle Dude a lacy fern,
and Surfing Kid's a red Geranium.
I've watched her stare at painful plants,
withhold her care, revengeful
when the break was hard.

The latest toy,
her Helicopter Boy
flew Huey Cobra Gunships
for "the Few, the Proud, the Brave."
To my surprise she talked of dinner introductions—
hesitated,
asked me to advise.

But then this morning found her crying,
cell phone at her side.
I sat down, prepared to sympathize.
("A plant is coming," I surmised.)
She looked at me,
and what she said gave him a name,
"Dad, Michael's dead.
Shot down last night."
And now, it's late at night
but I can't sleep.
I write my Congressman to ask
the worth of Michael's life,
what trade was made?
And does he know his name,
or was he OCCUPANT?

## The Franklin Sisters

They hunted ensigns from the choir loft,
fresh meat to lure their prey and legs that sprung
like steel traps, their nipples firm as bullets
when they finished off the job.  I could
not sing and preferred pagan gods in flowers,
trees, and other living things, so I
just watched as Tina captured Tom, who sold
his Porshe, bought a rock as big as Kansas,
which she flashed around, then bashed his crown
and stuffed his head and hung it in the den.
And then sweet Lisa Sue got Jim, and smothered
him until his brain was turned to mush
and she was left to lead him by a leash.
But Patty Beth was my downfall, with breasts
that pointed up and out and impish nose
that wrinkled when she laughed at me.  She promised
much with eyes, and smiles, and flaunted parts.
I left my gods and joined the choir to be
near her, then mouthed the hymns and faked the prayers.
Her Barbee breasts were steel-sharp.  She hooked
my lip, then ground me up and tossed me back
as chum to lure the bigger fish.  But then
her Catholic God collected all my pieces
up, and there I found a love of Jesus..

# William

I'm tired again.  Though I'm the boss I'm first
to start and last to leave, and gone most weeks
to small motels.  On doctor's threat I nurse
one coffee, though at work I sometimes sneak

a second cup.  It's secretary's day.
I'd better stop by Ralph's and buy a bunch
of flowers.  Maybe I can buy bouquets
at work from my laptop.  No time for lunch

today (again), I'd better grab a donut
on the way.  Oh shit!  I need to pay
that stack of bills, find time before they shut
the power off.  I've got to get away.

But then, think how much worse my life could be—
just watch poor Juan at work under that tree.

# Juan[xxii]

*(with thanks to Walt Whitman and William Carlos Williams)*

Behold this garden! I tend it well
That the marigolds dance in delight
under the caress of my hose,
That the snapdragons shout with bold strokes of color,
That the shy peonies blush
beneath their oversized Easter bonnets,
That the petunias branch forth in joyful abundance after the ecstasy of
pinched buds,
The flowers reach in joy to the sky and to my eyes.

Walk this orchard path!
It grows the raspberries along the fence, so tart and crunchy,
It gives the apples, peaches, oranges, grapefruits, pears
and all are good to the taste,
It gives the grapes, the red ones, and purple ones,
and green seedless ones,
And everything is mine to eat and share with birds,

It gives this plum

it is delicious
        so sweet
so cold.

This perfect spot!
Beneath this pungent pepper tree, I throw my shirt to the ground and sit,
Hear the man-made waterfall
as it laughs and plays with the rocks,
Hear the sparrows as they sing of their maker,
Hear the hawk overhead, riding the waves of air and sun,

Hear the wind blow music through this tree,
and all the trees around me,
And all things embrace me with their music.
Watch as poor Mr. William drives away,
the poor man who has given everything to me.

# Frank

No more than one hundred feet
from our driveway,
a thump and yelp.

I saw his dog pulling itself painfully,
slowly,
off to the side of the road
by it's front legs.

I called his dispatcher.
He was there in three minutes,
his car black and menacing,
the flashing lights silent,
his badge a beacon of authority.

I explained about his dog
and offered to help take the dog to the vet.
He looked through his sunglasses,
unsnapped his service revolver,
and said, "No, I'll put him down."

He didn't hesitate, or
cry, or hold the dog's head,
or look into his eyes one last time.

I saw his ex-wife yesterday,
with her wounded eyes,
and thought of him.

## Clive

A big guy, Clive, a ponytail slinked down
his slouching back,  I watched his Harley growl
for him, as mild men with balding crowns
will proudly walk their pit bulls, stare and scowl.

He slipped into his tattoo skin, then buckled
on his leather shell, protections from
the world of boys who pointed, chuckled, knuckled
crew cut hair.  He saw the world as scum

and carried knife and gun to wall away
the "they" that lurked and leered and laughed at him.
I often wondered why the vast array
of armor, battlements, and other grim

defenses holding others out, but when
the FBI arrested Clive for bombing
schools I realized his goal had been
locking in, controlling, ceaseless calming.

## John Might

By day John Might is "Mister Might," by night
he's just another guy in motel bar,
or working late on veneer desk, cigar
in hand, mini-bar beer in eight ounce glass
beside his Sony Laptop.  John is called
a hatchet man, but quietly.  To save
a failing company he tortures profits
from bleeding Excel sheets, while moving men
from cell to cell.  These five are saved, those ten
condemned, the price we pay to stay in play,
to keep the brand red hot.  It's not to say
he doesn't care, but someone's got to whip
them into shape.  It's just a job and John
is good at it.  He fires dozens here,
and there a dozen more, the iron fist
spares none.  We all feared him until the day
we found him dead, a bullet in his head.

## Blue Max

My broken car, Mercedes Benz, sustains
its speed but whistles when I fail to heed
the flapping fender's dents and rents.  I pull
into a tarnished yard, "Mack's Body Shop"
is faintly painted over rust atop
the corrugated dust, an office guarding
yards of broken cars, retired tires,
a dog that may be dead, or not.  The old
man squints suspicious eyes, peers at my pain,
writes on a clipboard, peers down again,
then asks, "Your name, that's German, right?", I nod,
he ponders, finally asks, "You step inside,

I show you something?" Cautiously I follow
him, and in the gloom of flashing dust
he pulls a flask of bourbon from behind
a Mobile drum.  He sets two glasses out
and gently rests a cigar box atop
his desk.  The cigar box holds photos, old
and cracked, and medals gleaming, seeming new
and menacing.  An Iron Cross, a Wound
Award, Luftwaffe Pilot decoration,
and a Blue Max.  "I shot down seventeen,"
he whispers, "now I hesitate, afraid
to tell, or show my mementos, and so
I hide and fix their broken cars and keep
my fame in cigar boxes.  You won't tell,
will you?" he pleads, then slumps.  I don't agree,
or disagree, but take the estimate,
turn and leave silence behind.  I step
past a dog that may be dead, or not.

## Jim Denison

The auctioneer's gavel banged, I'd saved
the storage shed contents.  Salvation sales
occupied my time, but, Christ, what junk.
A testament to people's hopeless faith
in resurrected fashions, born again
belongings, sin of waste avoided.  Home
I carted cardboard boxes,
sorted through the trash:
worn clothes and broken toys, chipped plates,
a family Bible, and old papers baptized
with the stain of seeping rain—a mount
of trash.  That night I sat by firelight,
sipped wine, and read those molded pages, poems
penned in scrawling hand by Denison.
Some were good, and some were bad,
but each portrayed
a bitter man and thankless world.
As pages turned a shape appeared,
not clear and sharp
but faded . . . dark.  Jim Denison
was sitting there.  I understood, or thought
I did, and said that
writing poems gave him immortality.
He shook his head,
looked "cross the room to stare at old belongings,
then blinked.  He said "You must read and believe."
I watched him fade, remained confused, and later
woke to realize it must have been
a dream.  I tossed the clothes and toys, the plates
and poems, hesitated with the Bible,
I don't know why, and then tossed that as well.

# The Book of Sevens, Part 2

## The Seven Heavenly Virtues

### Charity[xxiii]

In Africa ten dollars feeds two children
for a month, and educates them too;
Or water world-wide is fifty billion.
But now for more than that we overthrew
Saddam and bought Iraq. Let's give it back,
get a refund (we have receipts), and buy
goodwill with acts of charity. Attack
with kindness, using love to pacify.
In El Cajon ten dollars buys a movie,
but a Coke is more. While over dinner
we philosophize, sip wine and smoothly
save the world, because God loves a winner,
    or so it seems until that night, alone,
    my acts of charity postponed, postponed.

# Hope

My postponed acts of charity haunt me,
so I seek "virtue loopholes" for salvation,
and looking at the scope of hope I see
hope is "desire, belief, and expectation."
An easy one, this seems a surety,
for all men have desires, this I believe;
for gold, or sex, or racial purity
to list a few. And evil men achieve
evil with expectations of success.
I'll keep my wealth, and set high goals at work,
exploit the loophole, sneak past hell, unless
they audit me up there, Christ! Some fool clerk
 might look inside my heart, a shibboleth,
 and my shortcuts won't stop a fiery death.

## Justice

No legal tricks will stop a fiery death
for evil people, punished for their ways
as justice judges after their last breath.
But what is evil? Murder nowadays
may qualify. Except in war and gas
chambers. But what about crusades, and human
sacrifices to old gods? Those mass
murders were blessed by priests, whose acumen
and words were trusted by good men. Is evil
subjective? Something that varies through
the times? How can we judge acts in primeval
days with present codes? Or kill men who
     our leaders say must die, without concern
     that rules will change, and then we, too, might burn?

## Temperance

If only rules would change, and I might burn
the midnight oil, my bridges, with desire,
(and yes) my candle at both ends.  I yearn
to be the errant friar, the nasty choir
boy.  To hell with temperance, let's drink
cheap wine and fumble from our clothes, then stand
against my lighted bedroom window—pink
porn billboards for the cars that watch this banned,
unplanned sex show, your rosy nipples
pressed against the window pane.  Almost
I wish . . . but no, I can't.  I'm held by triple
chains of father, son and holy ghost.
     The fires beckon, threaten, even delude;
     shall I sin, or pray for fortitude?

## Fortitude[xxiv]

I pray for fortitude to face another
day, my thoughts as old as blackened snow.
MacDougall showed a soul has weight, and others
dangle heaven above, with hell below,
and purgatory some kind of safety net.
Fortitude saw Peter crucified
upside down, the cross a silhouette
against the human torches, glorified
and tar encased, and yes, their fortitude
helped see them through the martyrdom.  Extol
their death, but damn, it doesn't help my mood
to know they saved those twenty grams of soul.
    Perhaps this life's a path, death a doorway,
    but I think I'll squeeze joy from life today.

## Prudence

Though prudence says to squeeze joy from today,
it dictates what's okay, and what is wrong.
Seductions by that friend in lingerie,
were weighed—the pros and cons—so I stayed strong
and prudent, no affairs or casual sex.
I turned down bribes, some quite substantial, passed
on jobs with criminals.  And for complex
but prudent reasons put my yearnings last
and took that corporate job, held fast to needs
of family.  I led a cautious life,
a long contented life, this I'll concede.
I've buried all my friends, and mourned my wife.
    So now I sleep, read, rock, and slowly walk
    through snowy woods, and think what might have been.

## Faith

While in the snowy woods I think what might
have been.  I lost my faith at seventeen,
that is, that godly faith in wrong and right,
in or out.  I live somewhere between,
a world of doubt where falling snow makes ugly
bright, and covers beauty with its cold.
I'd dig below, but what's beneath lies snugly
waiting for rebirth.  I am consoled
with icy gems on lonely walks, at least
I say I am.  At home I roll a trail
to god from a ten dollar bill, released
from snorted snow that laughs as I inhale.
     In Africa this bill would help, it's true—
     two children fed and educated too.

# Resting Places

## Dinner at the Diner

I hold my paperback shield
while watching you wait.
The wine in your half empty glass
ripples in time with the steady kiss
of your finger tip tapping the rim
as your eyes stare at the door.

He enters with a rush of cold air,
and you look relieved,
then concerned
as he sits on the edge of his seat
speaking earnestly to you,
then leaves with the unmelted snow
still white on his blue woolen coat.

I look from your face, to the floor,
to my book, to your face and observe
the moistness of the eyes you blot with a napkin,
the trembling hand as you take a sip of water,
the short inhalations of breath.

You pick up your coat and purse.
I hide deeper in the safety of my chair,
turn back to my book and dinner,
and spend the evening deciding
what I should have said.

## Waltzing in San Marco's Square[xxv]

Moon over Venice,
the night warm and misty—
we waltzed to the music
in San Marco's Square.
The church in the background
watched over our waltzing;
the body of Mark
is buried in there.
We're floating on air
over cobblestone walkways,
watching the gondolas,
portals through time.
The merchants of Venice
still sell magic potions
to bring back romance
when it falters or fails.

## Hiking From Monterosso to Vernazza

The path steps up the steep mountain side.
My thighs burn with happy heat
as we climb
the flagstones set into the prominence.
On either side grow terraced rows of grapes,
green and purple,
intermingled with small tomatoes.
The path leads us through a banquet
of ripe blackberries, the bushes
extending their arms to say,
"You are my guest! Please! Enjoy!"
I savor the velvet texture,
the brief crunch of seeds,
the burst of flavor spiced with a hint of dust.
Stepping off the path into a small grotto,
we rest in the shade and dip our feet
into a pool of cool water, our toes dancing
in a tiny waterfall.  We sit back and listen
to the background music of the wind blowing
through the cave and the surrounding leaves.
A brown and gold butterfly alights
upon a delicate flower—
a tiny purple cornucopia.

## Swedish Sauna

We file into the sauna,
my employees excited to share their culture,
me regretting my bravado of the previous evening.
They sit on the cedar benches and talk,
without clothes,
I sit on the cedar bench and talk,
naked, stripped, exposed,
my hands and arms covering,
forced to my side, covering, crossed.
The heat enters my nostrils,
swirls inside my head,
sizzles from my scalp and bubbles in a sheen
of molten inhibition down my chest.
Thomas suggests they go easy on me,
my first time, and I nod.
We open the thick cedar door,
walk single file down the rough wooden planks.
The ice skaters ignore the pink gooseflesh parade
marching toward the hole in the ice.
I shrink from the cold and pretend
not to notice the flash
of my secretary's camera
as one by one we wave,
smile for the camera and drop
into the black water below.

## Nassau, Bahamas

I left the ship and found myself alone,
sidling through a ghetto scene, Chicago's
Cabrini Green came to my mind. You know
my sense: All black pebbles with one white stone.

But this was not a city slum, these men
and women owned this land. I was the one
who was afraid, a foolish fear begun
in prejudice I thought was done. And when

I looked past skin and finally saw the proud
women, with heads held high, and laughing men
who sat and talked on hand-hewn benches, then
all colors merged as one with bustling crowds.

# Corniglia Beach

I hop across the paving stones of hell
regurgitated over sand as white heat
sizzles soles this August day.
I look around, the rocks are firm,
their pointed tips protrude and poke, I struggle
past massive granite with dark cleavage,
boulder bosoms thrusting up
to gravel nipples.

The topless women glance my way, I start
to say something but then, I run my hand
through balding hair,
adjust my suit on my protruding gut,
remember I don't speak the language.

I toss the towel, hobble to the warm water,
and dwindle down upon a rock chaise lounge.
The surf rolls gently over me,
I pop a beer
and settle back to simply leer.

## Imusicapella

I lie in bed and listen to the sounds
swirling up from the Spanish Steps.
You sway naked on our hotel balcony,
communing with the vocal harmonies
of the Imusicapella gospel group.
Your breasts dance before the crowd,
an offering to the music of Moses Hogan,
and somehow, it isn't ironic.

# The Seventh Circle[xxvi]

I walk the paths around my home, and start
to north or south, but soon I'm here
beside route seven, trapped
where all paths circle back
to this tormenting trail through broken bottles,
beer cans, a faded tennis shoe.
Again I see that roadside cross.
I focus on a Black-Eyed-Susan,
watch it stare
and nod its yellow cheer. I stoop to sniff,
but then recall that these flowers smell bad,
a putrid stench as if they rotted underneath
their surface smiles.
My mind is drawn back to the cross,
recalling beers, a flash of cracked windshield,
and then a body rumbling overhead,
sounds like a dryer tumbling tennis shoes.

# The Book of Sevens, Part 3

## The Seven Sacraments

### Penance

Destroying humankind with massive floods
was once the penalty for rampant sins.
But Jesus died, and gave his flesh and blood
so priests could hear the sin, forgive, and then
the sinner could be reconciled with Christ.
Those early priests gave penance lasting years,
with public shame, animals sacrificed,
and bloodied knees before the monsignors.
Then seventh century Irish priests
began a new tradition in the parish—
confess in private weakness to the Beast,
a few Hail Marys, and your sins will perish.
    And now I hear of internet confessions
    forgiving you those little indiscretions.

# Matrimony

Forgiving you those little indiscretions
is how we've made it twenty-seven years.
And yes, I too have had my small transgressions
but each morning I look, and you're still here.
Because our marriage is a sacrament
we're a threesome, with God the faithful friend
whose steady love does more than just augment
good times.  When we were broken, He would mend
our hearts, our love, our minds.  But what of death?
Must death divorce us?  Jesus said there's no
marriage in heaven.  When my heart stops, breath
fails, and vision fades, must love also go?
    Before I'll spend eternity apart
    I'll sneak away with you to hell, Sweetheart.

## Extreme Unction

"I'll never sneak past hell.  God can't ignore
my sins." moaned the condemned inmate as he
prepared to die.  "Please father, I implore
you give last rights before the court's decree."
The priest sat down and slowly shook his head.
"Though death is certain, dawn will be here quickly,
(And yes, it's true you found the Lord)," he said
"I fear last rites are only for the sick."
The chair jolted, the lights flickered, the doctor
rushed in, he listened with his stethoscope,
then shouted out, "Heartbeat!"  The warden swore—
cried out, "We'll try again."  But forward loped
    the priest, who now gave last rights to the man,
    who gave his body up to death, per plan.

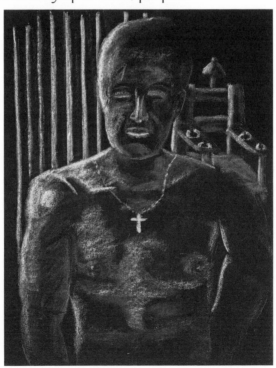

## Eucharist

"Who gave his body up to death, per plan?"
"Jesus," screamed the upturned faces learning
lessons.  Teachers telling tales began
preparing pupils who were eager, burning
for the holy wafers, youth enticed
to seek the spirit.  So like soma, used
by Hindus, or Greek nectar, we drink Christ's
blood and eat his flesh when bread's transfused.
Communion wafers must be made of wheat
I'm told.  No other grain will do. It's plain
to me the rules are somewhat incomplete—
Consider genetically altered grain.
    So genes created by mankind, converted,
    becoming Christ-like—seems somewhat perverted.

## Holy Orders

Becoming Christ-like seems somewhat perverted
to those who castigate the celibacy.
They think that priests are cloistered, introverted,
and jeopardize their righteous relevancy.
For me a priest portrays a local God.
With wisdom, patience—Christ's commands are heeded.
A priest is not a movie set facade,
more like insurance, comforting when needed.
I read a book that talked about the way
the hero met his priest weekly to play
a game of chess and wile the time away.
I envy casual closeness, not just Sunday
    masses held before the crowds, but fear
    of God restrains me yet another year.

## Confirmation

I'm still waiting for yet another year.
I strive each day, with varying success,
to teach them through example to revere
the Catholic faith, although I do confess
that in some way I must have failed—not one
of three offspring agrees to undertake
confirmation? What I forced, got done,
but confirmation's something I won't make
an adult do.  They talk of issues with
the Church, Eastern concepts, modern cults,
Roman myths, ancient monoliths.
But sleeping late on Sunday's the result.
     Their absence says that faith's superfluous.
     It seems as if they sleep to punish us.

## Baptism

Oh God, why must you punish us for those
faults of distant ancestors, those sins
in Eden long ago?  Sure Adam chose
to eat the apple then, but tell me when
this babe of mine has sinned, to need the cleansing
fluid from the font?   They say the water
brings the Holy Spirit, my offspring's
conscience. I tell you, how I raise my daughter
must mean more than this dash, this splash of liquid
when teaching her what's right and wrong.  Last, chrism
anoints her forehead, ears, mouth, and eyelids
ensuring heaven through Catholicism.
  At least it's not the Baptism of Blood
  Or killing human kind with massive floods.

# More Responses To the Dead

## Omar Khayam

### LI

*The moving finger writes; and, having writ,*
*moves on: nor all thy piety nor wit*
*  shall lure it back to cancel half a line,*
*nor all thy tears wash out a word of it.*

### Parody

My moving fingers type; and, having typed
press send.  My reply with the flames and gripes
  about my boss emailed to my friend.
"Reply All" copies both down network pipes.

# Alfred, Lord Tennyson

## Come Not, When I am Dead

*Come not, when I am dead,*
*To drop thy foolish tears upon my grave,*
*To trample round my fallen head,*
*And vex the unhappy dust thou wouldst not save.*
*There let the wind sweep and the plover cry;*
*But thou, go by.*
*Child, if it were thine error or thy crime*
*I care no longer, being all unblest:*
*Wed whom thou wilt, but I am sick of Time,*
*And I desire to rest.*
*Pass on, weak heart, and leave me where I lie:*
*Go by, go by.*

### The woman replies:

I wait, but you're not dead.
In fact, last night I saw you in the town,
a tramp on lap with her knees spread,
heaped food and drink and singing friends around.
I came to say your poem made me cry.
When will you die?
My friends all told me that I was a fool,
but I believed your flowers set in rhyme.
And when they said that you could be so cruel,
I thought they lied.  Now I'm
the victim of your verse.  So my reply?
Just die, just die.

# Walter Savage Landor

## Well I Remember

*Well I remember how you smiled*
*To see me write your name upon*
*The soft sea-sand . . . "O! what a child!*
*You think you're writing upon stone!"*
*I have since written what no tide*
*Shall ever wash away, what men*
*Unborn shall read o'er ocean wide*
*And find Ianthe's name again.*

## Response

While browsing through a swap meet nook
I found your poem almost dead
and hiding in a ten-cent book
and thought you had a swollen head,
to think your verse would last through time
and keep Ianthe's name alive.
But I'll help out, because my rhyme
will last as long as men survive.

# Robert Herrick

## To the Virgins

Gather ye rosebuds while ye may,
   Old time is still a-flying:
And this same flower that smiles to-day
   To-morrow will be dying.

The glorious lamp of heaven, the sun,
   The higher he's a-getting,
The sooner will his race be run,
   And nearer he's to setting.

That age is best which is the first,
   When youth and blood are warmer;
But being spent, the worse, and worst
   Times still succeed the former.

Then be not coy, but use your time,
   And while ye may go marry:
For having lost but once your prime
   You may for ever tarry.

## The Virgin Replies

Married and pregnant while a teen
no time was left for schooling.
I thought a child would simply mean
a rosy face a-cooing.

The glorious joy of nursing my son
is fading, he's a-getting
into my brain, a screaming gun
that maims without bloodletting.

My husband helped a bit at first
but as the work grew endless,
his eyes accused, his manner cursed,
he claimed we made him friendless.

I lost the bloom of my childhood
following your advice.
You should have said that waiting's good,
but men don't pay the price.

# George Gordon, Lord Byron

## She Walks in Beauty

She walks in beauty, like the night
Of cloudless climes and starry skies;
And all that's best of dark and bright
Meet in her aspect and her eyes:
Thus mellowed to that tender light
Which heaven to gaudy day denies.

One shade the more, one ray the less,
Had half impaired the nameless grace
Which waves in every raven tress,
Or softly lightens o'er her face;
Where thoughts serenely sweet express
How pure, how dear their dwelling-place.

And on that cheek, and o'er that brow,
So soft, so calm, yet eloquent,
The smiles that win, the tints that glow,
But tell of days in goodness spent,
A mind at peace with all below,
A heart whose love is innocent!

## Parody and Response

She walks the streets long past midnight,
hangs out in gay and gothic bars.
She wears short skirts, or pants too tight,
eats greasy fries, not caviar,
but she's my only love despite
her tendency to hop in cars.

She doesn't mind, gives me a piece,
although she knows I cannot pay,
and when she gives me that release
in doorways or in alleyways
I know it's love, for I'm obese
and yet she's friendly anyway.

Perhaps my girl is not like yours,
so perfect and so high-faloot,
a Barbie doll that doesn't snore
or sweat or shit or prostitute,
but still I think I love her more
than some romantic absolute.

# John Keats

## Ode on a Grecian Urn

*Thou still unravished bride of quietness,*
*Thou foster child of silence and slow time,*
*Sylvan historian, who canst thus express*
*A flowery tale more sweetly than our rhyme:*
*What leaf-fringed legend haunts about thy shape*
*Of deities or mortals, or of both,*
*In Tempe or the dales of Arcady?*
*What men or gods are these? What maidens loath?*
*What mad pursuit? What struggle to escape?*
*What pipes and timbrels? What wild ecstasy?*

*Heard melodies are sweet, but those unheard*
*Are sweeter; therefore, ye soft pipes, play on;*
*Not to the sensual ear, but, more endeared,*
*Pipe to the spirit ditties of no tone.*
*Fair youth, beneath the trees, thou canst not leave*
*Thy song, nor ever can those trees be bare;*
*Bold Lover, never, never canst thou kiss,*
*Though winning near the goal—yet, do not grieve;*
*She cannot fade, though thou hast not thy bliss*
*Forever wilt thou love, and she be fair!*

*Ah, happy, happy boughs! that cannot shed*
*Your leaves, nor ever bid the Spring adieu;*
*And, happy melodist, unwearied,*
*Forever piping songs forever new;*
*More happy love! more happy, happy love!*
*Forever warm and still to be enjoyed,*
*Forever panting, and forever young;*
*All breathing human passion far above,*
*That leaves a heart high-sorrowful and cloyed,*
*A burning forehead, and a parching tongue.*

*Who are these coming to the sacrifice?*
*To what green altar, O mysterious priest,*
*Lead'st thou that heifer lowing at the skies,*

160

*And all her silken flanks with garlands dressed?*
*What little town by river or sea shore,*
*    Or mountain-built with peaceful citadel,*
*        Is emptied of this folk, this pious morn?*
*And, little town, thy streets for evermore*
*    Will silent be; and not a soul to tell*
*        Why thou art desolate, can e'er return.*
*O Attic shape! Fair attitude! with brede*
*    Of marble men and maidens overwrought,*
*With forest branches and the trodden weed;*
*    Thou, silent form, dost tease us out of thought*
*As doth eternity. Cold Pastoral!*
*    When old age shall this generation waste,*
*        Thou shalt remain, in midst of other woe*
*Than ours, a friend to man, to whom thou say'st,*
*    "Beauty is truth, truth beauty"—that is all*
*        Ye know on earth, and all ye need to know.*

## The Bride Replies

You fool! You thought I ran to remain chaste,
and praised the fact that now I'm never caught.
In fact, I ran so I could be embraced
by panting love without disgrace. Who thought

my scheme would leave me without love, to live
a life of loneliness? Those melodies
you think the piper plays? They're squawks that give
us all headaches. His tutor's gone, and these

bleeps are all he knows. As for the poor
old priest and cow? He lost his faith ages ago
as his gods were replaced by Christ and your
world's trinity. We thought you'd like to know

that beauty without change is false and dies,
for true beauty is in change and surprise.

161

## Walt Whitman Visits Again

### A Hand-Mirror

*Hold it up sternly—see this it sends back, (who is it?  is it you?)*
*Outside fair costume, within ashes and filth,*
*No more a flashing eye, voice, hands, step,*
*A drunkard's breath, unwholesome eater's face, venerealee's flesh,*
*Lungs rotting away piecemeal, stomach sour and cankerous,*
*Joints rheumatic, bowels clogged with abomination,*
*Blood circulating dark and poisonous streams,*
*Words babble, hearing and touch callous,*
*No brain, no heart left, no magnetism of sex;*
*Such from one look in this looking glass ere you go hence,*
*Such a result so soon—and from such a beginning!*

## Response

Oh Walt, I've got to say this is not you,
these cannot really be your words.  It's true

they say you wrote this piece, and yet the mood
is more like reading Baudelaire.  No lewd

or celebrating song, but bitter, dark
and putrid thoughts grow from this page, pockmark

this piece.  And you should know that while you rot,
and feed the grass you loved so much, you're not

dead yet.  Your words inspire and guide, free verse
that flows like mountain streams which fall, traverse

the rocky slopes then surge through hidden glade
to nurture poets sheltered in your shade.

# Thomas Hardy

## A Broken Appointment

*You did not come,*
*And marching Time drew on, and wore me numb—*
*Yet less for loss of your dear presence there*
*Than that I thus found lacking in your make*
*That high compassion which can overbear*
*Reluctance for pure loving kindness' sake*
*Grieved I, when, as the hope-hour stroked its sum,*
*You did not come.*

*You love not me,*
*And love alone can lend you loyalty;*
*I know and knew it.  But, unto the store*
*Of human deeds divine in all but name,*
*Was it not worth a little hour or more*
*To add yet this:  Once you, a woman, came*
*To soothe a time-torn man; even though it be*
*You love not me?*

## Response

She did not come,
But going on and on is somewhat dumb.
I mean, I like this piece, its poignant mood,
And poetry to get revenge is cool,
But nowadays we say, "Get past it, dude!"
And real friends tell you when you are a fool,
So even if you thought she was a plum,
She did not come.

So let it be.
I know that you believed in deities,
That shape the universe in some strange way,
But calling pity meetings "deeds divine,"
Seems like a cheap attempt to get a lay.
I hope it worked.  If not, recall the line
About the other fish that swim at sea.
And let it be.

## William Blake

### The Sick Rose

*O Rose, thou art sick!*
*The Invisible worm,*
*That flies in the night,*
*In the howling storm,*

*Has found out thy bed*
*Of Crimson joy;*
*And his dark secret love*
*Does thy life destroy.*

## Parody

O Rose, thou art sick!
You drank the worm,
Tequila with lime,
In that rowdy bar,

And woke up in bed
With some cowboy.
Oh, your bright open love
will thy life destroy!

# William Cullen Bryant

## Mutation

*They talk of short—lived pleasure—be it so—*
*Pain dies as quickly: stem, hard-featured pain*
*Expires, and lets her weary prisoner go.*
*The fiercest agonies have shortest reign;*

*And after dreams of horror, comes again*
*The welcome morning with its rays of peace.*
*Oblivion, softly wiping out the stain,*
*Makes the strong secret pangs of shame to cease.*

*Remorse is virtue's root; its fair increase*
*Are fruits of innocence and blessedness:*
*Thus joy, o'erborne and bound, doth still release*
*His young limbs from the chains that round him press.*

*Weep not that the world changes—did it keep*
*A stable changeless state, "twere cause indeed to weep.*

## Response

I read this and I think, "This too shall pass"
has been a valid lesson since the time
of Solomon at least. Yes, verse has class,
and yet, the same message just set to rhyme.

I like your turn in which you seem to show
that change is good, that static states are cause
to weep. I guess I think that's so, although
much change today is no cause for applause.

Let's take divorce. It used to be a sin
and couples stayed together out of fear
of being ostracized. And men were men,
while wives stayed home, cleaned house, made meals, fetched beer.

But changing times now say my wife can split.
I liked it more when she had to submit.

# Robert Frost

## Stopping by the Woods on a Snowy Evening

*Whose woods these are I think I know,*
*His house is in the village though,*
*He will not see me stopping here*
*To watch his woods fill up with snow.*

*My little horse must think it queer*
*To stop without a farmhouse near*
*Between the woods and frozen lake*
*The darkest evening of the year.*

*He gives his harness bells a shake*
*To ask if there is some mistake*
*The only other sound's the sweep*
*Of easy wind and downy flake.*

*The woods are lovely, dark and deep,*
*But I have promises to keep,*
*And miles to go before I sleep,*
*And miles to go before I sleep.*

## Parody: Stopped by Freeway Traffic on a Snowy Evening

I planned for traffic, stop-and-go,
But that was in the city though,
And normally by here it's clear
But then there's all this gosh darn snow.

Today I noticed Jimmy's rear,
When after work we had a beer,
And Sue called Jim a real beefcake.
I wonder if that makes me queer?

I think I'm getting a headache.
That second beer was a mistake.
I shift and squeeze my knee to knee,
I stop, then go, give gas, then break.

If I could stop I'd piss a sea,
But I have no way to break free,
And miles to go before I pee,
And miles to go before I pee.

# John Donne

## Death

*Death be not proud, though some have called thee*
  *Mighty and dreadful, for, thou art not so,*
  *For, those, whom thou think'st, thou dost overthrow,*
  *Die not, poor death, nor yet canst thou kill me;*

  *From rest and sleep, which but thy pictures be,*
  *Much pleasure, then from thee, much more must flow,*
  *And soonest our best men with thee do go,*
  *Rest of their bones, and souls delivery.*

  *Thou'art slave to Fate, chance, kings, and desperate men,*
  *And dost with poison, war, and sicknesses dwell,*
  *And poppy, or charms can make us sleep as well,*
  *And better then they stroke; why swell'st thou then?*

  *One short sleep past, we wake eternally,*
  *And death shall be no more, Death thou shalt die.*

## Death Replies

Where are you now, John Donne?  It's your old friend,
and I was wondering how you felt now?
You laughed at me in poetry, I bow
to clever jests.  And yet, let's not pretend

that words you penned could make them laugh at me.
If I'm so weak, like sleep, then why not show
them proof that you were right so long ago.
I'm calling you old man!  I'll count to three

and then I'm giving up.  God damn it John,
wake up!  Just as I thought, no sign, no word,
I think you're really gone for good, absurd
of you to claim that I am just a con.

No John, you're just a corpse.  Your best bet now?
The Shakespeare way—eternal life through verse.

# William Wordsworth

## I Wandered Lonely As a Cloud

*I wandered lonely as a cloud*
*That floats on high o'er vales and hills,*
*When all at once I saw a crowd,*
*A host, of golden daffodils;*
*Beside the lake, beneath the trees,*
*Fluttering and dancing in the breeze.*

*Continuous as the stars that shine*
*And twinkle on the milky way,*
*They stretched in never-ending line*
*Along the margin of a bay:*
*Ten thousand saw I at a glance,*
*Tossing their heads in sprightly dance.*

*The waves beside them danced; but they*
*Out-did the sparkling waves in glee:*
*A poet could not but be gay,*
*In such a jocund company:*
*I gazed and gazed but little thought*
*What wealth the show to me had brought:*

*For oft, when on my couch I lie*
*In vacant or in pensive mood,*
*They flash upon that inward eye*
*Which is the bliss of solitude;*
*And then my heart with pleasure fills,*
*And dances with the daffodils.*

174

## Response


I like the way your daffodils
come to your mind and fill your heart
with pleasures of remembered hills
as told in sing-song lyric art
of metered verse and perfect rhyme,
which grows on me time after time.

But those inversions have to go,
just look at "saw I at a glance,"
who talks like that? Yes, yes I know
it keeps the flow, the poem's dance,
and helps end rhymes. Are you adverse
to moving this into free verse?

And then I think that it's too long,
compression is the key, and here
so many stanzas for a song
about some flowers, atmosphere
and such. I'd say delete S2
for sure, and maybe S3 too.

And then, it's just a bit cliche,
and much is rather abstract, so
there's lots that you can cut away
and stop the telling, start to show
and then you'll have a worthwhile piece.
I'm anxious for your next release.

# Reader Notes

[i]  Although most of this is written in iambic pentameter, the final stanza is properly read in "marching cadence" where anapests dominate and the stress corresponds with the right foot hitting the pavement, as follows:

I - knew a GAL - who was DRESSED - in RED,

SHE - had a PARK-ing meter- ON - her BED.

[ii]  "yellowjackets" is a reference both to the "stinging" aircraft but also to the yellow shirts on the flight deck. Yellow shirts direct aircraft during the moving, launching and landing of aircraft on the flight deck using a series of hand gestures to communicate with pilots and other flight deck personnel.

[iii]  Astral dreaming involves first controlling your dreams and ultimately, projecting yourself out of your body while dreaming.

[iv]  In the Unix operating system, when the operating system encounters an error from which it cannot recover that error is called a fatal error. When this happens the operating system creates a file that is a snapshot of it's internal memory at the moment it failed.

[v]  A poem about fading hearing, an occupational hazard of jet pilots.

[vi]  The "old man in the distance" is literally the narrator as old age comes over him and his death approaches.

[vii]  Another poem about death.

[viii]  Here the whirlpool in the above ground pool represents death, and the journey to the unknown that is through the tunnel.

[ix]  To me, there is something terrifying, fascinating, and peaceful (all at once) to the anonymity that death brings.

[x]  Qandisa: (Morocco) Female demon who seduces handsome young men and drives them insane.

xi  A pub can be a safe retreat, or a source of destruction for an alcoholic.

xii  The San Diego Wild Animal park is a "zoo" where the animals run free and the people are "caged" on controlled paths or in trams. It occurred to me that in a similar manner the "wild animals" of the homeless are free while the rest of us are caged in our controlled environment.

xiii  In honor of my mother, who like most mothers was fond of saying "If your friends jumped off a cliff, would you?"

xiv  Walt Whitman was a famous poet of the 19th century, writing free flowing verse, often about nature. His only book of poetry was called Leaves of Grass and he was openly gay.

xv  Buying the motorcycle resulted in my being kicked out of my home (expelled from Eden).

xvi  This poem is about dreams versus reality, with the woman's interjections pulling the narrator back to reality. He sees the nobility in her dress (and her), but she pulls him back to the reality that she is a prostitute. He sees flower waterfalls, but the reality is that the cafe Schober (in Zurich) is filled with plastic flowers. He sees the two of them in a Monet painting, she pulls him back to the reality that they are in a cafe. Finally, he begins to feel guilt about being in a cafe with a prostitute, and she reminds him that this is all just a poem, and not reality.

xvii  Pompeii was a Roman get-away location near Rome which was buried almost instantaneously by hot ash from a nearby volcano, leaving molds of the people (and animals) in lifelike action. In Pompeii brothels men would sit at a bar drinking wine while prostitutes walked past an open window behind the bar, trying to coax them upstairs. Roman vomitoriums were rooms near banquet facilities where gorged diners would throw up their meal so that they could continue eating more.

xviii  The quote is from a famous poem by Dylan Thomas.

xix  The phrase that "stage terms are from the point of view of actors, not the audience" is drilled into all actors from early in their training. In a similar manner, the life of our children as they grow older is from their point of view, not ours.

xx Here the abstract concept of "love" is made tangible as something that can be left "lying around" when it is embodied in things like made up beds and gourmet meals.

xxi E coli are the good bacteria in our intestines that help in digestion.

xxii Most of the poem is in the style of Walt Whitman, but the short section in the middle parodies "The Plum Apology" by William Carlos Williams.

xxiii Fifty billion dollars is the World Bank estimate of the cost to bring drinking water to every person in the world that does not currently have drinking water.

xxiv In 1907, Dr. Duncan MacDougall published his work in the journal American Medicine in which he showed that the weight of a human soul is approximately 20 grams. His experiments involved monitoring weight changes in patients immediately upon death. St. Peter was crucified by the Roman Emporer in the Emperor's courtyard. At his request, he was crucified upside down as a deference to Christ's crucifixion right-side up. At the same time, many Christians were covered in tar and burned alive as "living candles".

xxv This is designed to be read with a waltz-like rhythm.

xxvi In Dante's divine comedy, the seventh circle within the inferno was where those who killed others were forced to spend eternity. Black-eyed-susan are a daisy-like flower common around the roads in San Diego, which are very pretty but exude a foul odor when picked.

# Order your copy of
# The Giant Book of Poetry
## today.

## Authors include:

Patience Agbabi
Anna Akhmatova
Claribel Alegria
Agha Shahid Ali
Anonymous
Petronius Arbiter
Archilochos
Margaret Atwood
W.H. Auden
Amiri Baraka (LeRoi Jones)
Charles Baudelaire
David Berman
Charles Bernstein
The Bible
Elizabeth Bishop
Lucian Blaga
William Blake
Louise Bogan
Emily Bronte
Rupert Brooke
Gwendolyn Brooks
Elizabeth Barret
Browning
Robert Browning
Sharon Bryan
William Cullen Bryant
David Budbill
Robert Burns
George Gordon, Lord Byron
Thomas Campion
Thomas Carew
Lewis Carroll
Hayden Carruth

Kate Clanchy
William Cullen Bryant
Andrei Codrescu
Samuel Taylor Coleridge
Billy Collins
William Congreve
Nancy Vieira Couto
Abraham Cowley
Mark Cox
Stephen Crane
Robert Creeley
Jim Daniels
Toi Derricotte
Nuala Ni Dhomhnaill
James Dickey
Emily Dickinson
Thomas Disch
Stephen Dobyns
John Donne
Keith Douglas
Michael Drayton
William Drummond
Alan Dugan
Stuart Dybek
T.S. Eliot
Black Elk
Ralph Waldo Emerson
B.H. Fairchild
Irving Feldman
Eugene Field
Molly Fisk
Jane Flanders
Jorie Graham

Robert Frost
Gu Gheng
Lorna Goodison
Robert Greene
Eamon Grennan
Thom Gunn
Donald Hall
Mark Halliday
Thomas Hardy
Kaylin Haught
Seamus Heaney
Robert Hedin
Ernest Hemingway
William Ernest Henley
Tom Hennen
Robert Herrick
Oliver Wendell Holmes
Jackleen Holton
Thomas Hood
Gerard Manley Hopkins
Horace
A.E. Housman
David Huddle
Langston Hughes
David Ignatow
Mark Irwin
Wen I-to
Randall Jarrell
Robinson Jeffers
Louis Jenkins
Jokun (助菫)
Richard Jones
Roberto Juarroz

Donald Justice
Julia Kasdorf
John Keats
Brigit Pegeen Kelly
Miyazawa Kenji
Omar Khayam
Joyce Kilmer
Charles Kingsley
Galway Kinnell
Robert Kinsley
Rudyard Kipling
Carolyn Kizer
Etheridge Knight
Yusef Komunyakaa
Ted Kooser
Rutger Kopland
Walter Savage  Landor
Sidney Lanier
Philip Larkin
D.H. Lawrence
Robert Lax
Edward Lear
Li-Young Lee
Denise Levertov
Philip Levine
Larry Levis
Vachel Lindsay
Gerald Locklin
Henry Wadsworth
Longfellow
Richard Lovelace
Amy Lowell
Archibald MacLeish
Edgar Lee Masters
William Matthews
Gail Mazur
Heather McHugh
Edna St. Vincent Millay
John Milton
Adrian Mitchell
Marianne Moore
Moritake
Lisel Mueller

Jack Myers
James B Naylor
Howard Nemerov
William Butler Yeats
Alden Nowlan
Sean O'Brien
Sharon Olds
Mary Oliver
Wilfred Owen
Heberto Padilla
Dan Pagis
Coventry Patmore
Brian Patten
Michael Pettit
Robert Phillips
Robert Pinsky
Li Po
Edgar Allan Poe
Ezra Pound
Edwin Arlington
Robinson
William Roetzheim
Roka
Christina Georgina Rossetti
Timothy Russell
Ryusui
Carl Sandburg
Izet Sarajlic
Philip Schultz
Ruth Schwartz
Marjorie Allen Seiffert
Robert Service
Anne Sexton
William Shakespeare
Percy Bysshe Shelley
Richard Shelton
Mei Sheng
(Masaoka Tsunenori) Shiki
Tanikawa Shuntaro
Sir Philip Sidney
Edward Rowland Sill
Charles Simic
David Slavitt

Stevie Smith
Gary Snyder
Robert Southey
William Stafford
Maura Stanton
Gertrude Stein
Charles Perkins Stetson
Wallace Stevens
Robert Louis Stevenson
Richard Henry Stoddard
Mark Strand
Sir John Suckling
Joyce Sutphen
May Swenson
Sara Teasdale
Alfred, Lord Tennyson
Dylan Thomas
Shu Ting
Mark Turpin
Louis Untermeyer
Diane Wakoski
Derek Walcott
Ronald Wallace
William Walsh
Tom Wayman
Bruce Weigl
Walt Whitman
John Greenleaf Whittier
Richard Wilbur
Ella Wheeler Wilcox
C.K.Williams
William Carlos Williams
William Wordsworth
Sir Henry Wotton
James Wright
William Butler Yeats
Dean Young
Tao Yuan-ming
Adam Zabajewski
Zawgee
Paul Zimmer

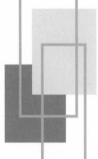

# ORDER FORM

## (all prices are in U.S. dollars for shipment to the United States)

| Description | Price | Quantity |
|---|---|---|
| The Giant Book of Poetry | | |
| Perfect Bound | $29.95 | |
| Leather Bound | $79.95 | |
| Thoughts I Left Behind | | |
| Perfect Bound | $14.95 | |
| Leather Bound | $79.95 | |
| The Giant Book Of Poetry Audio Book | | |
| Poems of Romance | $9.95 | |
| Poems of Romance (with subscription) | $0.49 | |
| | | |
| Shipping and Handling $4.95 plus $1.00 per book or CD ordered beyond 1 | | |
| Sales Tax for orders shipping to California | Add 7.75% | |

Your name

Address

Address

City, State Zip

Phone Number

Email Address

CHARGE INFORMATION

Credit card number

Credit card type: (Visa, Mastercard)

Expiration Date

Name on card if different from above

Billing zip code if different from above

Fax order form to: (619) 374-7311

or Mail photocopy of form to Level 4 Press, 13518 Jamul Drive, Jamul, CA 91935-1635

or visit our web site at *www.Level4Press.com* to place your order on-line.

# Meet me at the Poetry Coffeeshop!

COME VISIT
THE POETRY COFFEESHOP TO:

- Discuss the poems in this book;

- Post your own poems for comment;

- Discuss any topic related to poetry.

MEMBERSHIP IS FREE.

## www.PoetryCoffeeShop.com